T0065380

EARLY MORNING THOUGHTS

ROMAINE BELGROVE

authorHOUSE

AuthorHouse™
1663 Liberty Drive
Bloomington, IN 47403
www.authorhouse.com
Phone: 833-262-8899

Published by AuthorHouse 01/28/2021

ISBN: 978-1-6655-1138-4 (sc)
ISBN: 978-1-6655-1137-7 (e)

Library of Congress Control Number: 2020925132

Print information available on the last page.

OUR MOTHER

It is truly a blessing, to have a mother like you,
Who has always been there, when we weren't sure what to do.
There is nothing in this world, that could replace you,
Only God knows, where we would be without you.

You are a very generous person, who shared with everybody,
Even when you knew, they were thinking ill will of your family.
Always giving, down to your very last,
And not holding any grudge, or a wrongfully done past.

If nothing else, you made sure we had love,
Always showered us with it, like God up above.
What else in the world, could we ask for,
Than the love and attention we got from our mother.

Just like others, we did wrong things too,
And you would always correct us and show us the right thing to do.
A lot of that, is not happening these days,
As parents are not teaching kids, about respectful ways.

Whether you were there or not, we had no choice,
But to respect others, and not raise our voice.
Because that would attract, a very serious scolding,
And if it happened too often, then came the spanking.

What you passed on to us, was what you got from your own mother,
Oh, so loving, kind hearted and tender.
We never had to get licks growing up as children,
Because when elders spoke, everyone listened back then.

As expected, you have now grown older and not so strong,
But you are still with us, for however more long.
Just like the fighter, you have always been,
Tougher and stronger than any other known being.

We have grown in a way, that many others only dreamed of,
And you always showed, equal love among all of us.
We know you are still thinking of us, even on this slippery road,
And we all also love and adore you...Eugene, Aldorna, Belgrove.

SIBLING LOVE

All through the years it was always me and you,
When others had both mother and father, it was just us two.
But that never stopped us from being happy,
As we had the love of a soulful granny.

Life back then, was oh so rough,
But you always did your best and never gave up on us.
From being at home and helping with the chores,
To always looking out for me, at the sea shores.

We were very poor but always had something to eat,
And sometimes the torn shoes, barely covered our feet.
It didn't matter, because we had each other,
And going to school, was something worth waking up for.

Even tho', you were always two grades forward,
Having a protective big sister, never seemed awkward.
You didn't allow anyone, to take advantage of me,
And when I got stuck, you never left me alone in that tree.

Most children looked forward, to going away for summer,
But our only wish, was to stay as long as possible in the sea water.
Even when the rain came down, and I hid under a boat with fright,
You and the others laughed, but you never let me out of your sight.

I have other brothers and sisters, whom I love equally,
And its not a competition, but I love you dearly.
And you have shown me, that the feeling is mutual,
Always helping with my tasks, even when you feel a bit dull.

It's never too much, whenever I ask for your assistance,
Either help with my poems, or just a prayer for my very existence.
You never turn me away and say that you don't have time,
And if I ever needed it, you'd give your last dime.

What we have as siblings, is oh so precious,
No amount of quarrel, or had time, could ever come between us,
If there's even been anyone, to love others genuinely without reason,
It's my precious sister, Kilene Belgrove Richardson.

A CARIBBEAN CHRISTMAS

At some point in life we were all little girls or boys,
And Christmas just meant, getting new toys.
Some got more than enough and they were very happy,
While some of us never even saw a leaf of a Christmas tree.

That didn't stop us from enjoying ourselves,
We played and appreciated each other, just like everybody else.
Proving that Christmas, is not about gifts and wealth,
But most importantly, family and good health.

The scent of the turkey baking we can't soon forget,
We sat right there watching the oven, even though it made us sweat.
Don't even talk about, that dripping delicious ham,
We just wanted it, even in our little hands.

Nowhere else in the world has more food served at Christmas,
Once in the Caribbean, you eat till you ready to buss.
Pies, stuffing, relish and everything nice,
Don't forget our famous traditional, pigeon peas rice.

Have some sorrel, ginger beer or fruit punch,
But save some room because we don't just serve lunch.
We go all out and also serve desert,
A Caribbean Christmas is the best here on earth.

If you traveled from states and grandma asks, why you look like that?
Bet your sweet life you going back looking fat.
Because in these parts grandparents don't play,
They will feed you morning, noon and night every day.

Folklore through the streets was always something grand,
No one else can compare to our caroling throughout the land.
We also acknowledge, the true meaning of Christmas,
Which is that Christ came and died for all of us.

We understand that those days are long gone by,
But to bring back the true meaning, let us at least try.
And do what we did so many years ago,
That's making the Caribbean Christmas, the
best the world may ever know.

A NURSE'S LIFE

Although you may not see, the reflection in your purse,
Am sure in life, you preferred nothing more than to be a nurse.
It's a very tough job, but someone has to do it,
So doing it just for the money, is like an athlete entering a race unfit.

Every day you leave your home to go and do this job,
Which gets so tough at times, that you were ready to sob.
But it's by your own will and determination,
That you so able and willingly serve your nation.

Every single job has value in its own way,
Still it takes an extra special person to be a nurse day after day.
You didn't sign up for this job because it was the only one available,
But because of your passion, to help the sick and disable.

Not even a busy New York day with bumper to bumper traffic,
Can compare to the things you see daily, which can be real graphic.
From a simple scratch, cut or even a broken leg,
To severe chest pains, or a gunshot wound to the head.

Sometimes you needed to close your eyes for a five,
But had to keep them open, in order to keep someone else alive.
Because while others are out partying waiting for a lift,
You are behind a desk, working the graveyard shift.

The sight and smell of blood and medication,
Can make the average person turn and run without hesitation.
So imagine having to face that every single day,
In my opinion nurses should be in the top 3 when it comes to pay.

Sometimes no help is available to help shift a patient on a bed,
And the weight is twice as much when you find out the patient is dead.
Instead of throwing up your hands and saying not you,
The prayers flow from your mouth, and you did what you could do.

There are so many things we could say about these wonderful women,
All I know is that they were sent from heaven.
So whenever there's consideration for National Heroes Day,
It's about time a nurse was nominated, what do you say?

ALPHONSO BRIDGEWATER

Who is this guy that everyone in Solid Waste speaks so highly about?
Who is able to get a whole conversation out
of you without opening his mouth.
Make sure when you speak you say all that's on your mind,
Because when it's his turn he'll tell you wait a minute you had your time.

Employees would often go to him and complain,
While cool and calm he just sits and wonder
what's going through their brain.
Allowing you to talk and do your own thing,
Then at the opportune moment he says, "but here's the thing."

Don't think he's being harsh and not paying attention,
It's just his way of asking, "Is there anything you forgot to mention?"
Be it work related, personal or you're just feeling ill,
He was our very own local Dr. Phil.

His affiliation in sports made him even easier to deal with,
He's now way past that but still thinks he can
win a race after eating a sandwich.
Never bragging, or boasting of his accomplishments,
Luckily in his days of football he never sat on the bench.

He's a well-rounded athlete who took part in all sorts of sports,
Don't judge him by his size, he even played on
the basketball and tennis courts.
He was always slim built in bodily structure,
But am sure we all know the saying don't judge a book by its cover.

He settled into Solid Waste Management
Corporation some 20 years ago,
During which he paved the way from yesterday
till today and for tomorrow.
Each day on the job, was a new challenge for him,
But was conquered easily as you could tell from his grin.

You can't tell, when he's having a bad day,
Because no matter what he'll always listen to what you have to say.
Then try his best to find a solution,
Even if he ends up saying that you full of confusion.

Tried, tested and proven he passed all the tests,
No one can argue when I say as our Manager, he was simply the best.
I am not being biased, and I still want the best for our future,
But I still have to say, there'll never be another
ALPHONSO BRIDGEWATER.

APPRECIATE LIFE

You woke up this morning to see another day,
But did you remember, to look to the sky and pray.
We can't be too busy to thank the one up above,
Who blesses us every day with tender mercy and love.

Some say, they don't believe in God,
But whenever trouble arises, first thing you hear is, oh Lord.
It's not right to call upon Him, at our convenience,
Living without Christ, is like not having a conscience.

Wife love your husbands and husbands love your wife,
But don't you dare forget, the one who gave you both life.
We might say, we came from our mother,
But she also came, from the greatest creator.

We often find time, for just about anything,
But what about that man, who opened your eyes this morning.
Do you even find time, just to say thanks?
Or just run to your stove and start cooking franks.

All the hustling and bustling, that we often do,
At the end of the day, still won't save me and you.
Unless we acknowledge, who's the real reason,
That we can be here for each and every season.

It should be an honor to once again be alive,
To look at those honey bees, showing appreciation for their hive.
Or what about, those birds flying so high,
If they had one wing, they would never be in the sky.

God gifted us, with what we know as nature,
So why not use it, to make our lives better.
Instead of trying, to see who makes the biggest bombs.
Because pushing one button, could destroy all our lungs.

So again, I say, to each and every nation,
Take a serious look at life, and start showing appreciation.
So that, when we depart this life instead of sobbing goodbyes,
Those left behind can rejoice, because we've now
gone to appreciate, a new life in the skies.

BORN TO HELP OTHERS

Taking your time, effort, money and resources to help others,
Dealing with the sisters who in turn would help our brothers,
It's something you do to try and help your country,
You give every effort without looking back for money.

It comes with hard work and lots of perseverance,
You're a strong black woman who does good
without looking for an audience.
Pushing on with the strong will passed on from your father,
You're already an inspiration to plenty of less fortunate mothers.

There are those who don't see the value of what you're doing,
But no matter what the good lord will bless your every bidding.
With the limited resources you still keep on doing it,
It's kind of hard on you but I know you will never quit.

Lots of women out there are depending on you,
Push on my sister just keep doing your do.
There's a saying, a bad wind never blows,
Man can hide from each other but the lord always knows.

All in time you'll see your blessing come true,
I have every confidence in this and I know you do too.
We all have our time when we feel a little pain,
But time heals all wounds, so be strong **Mrs. Etsu Bradshaw Caines**.

DEPLOY DON'T DESTROY

One of our worst nightmares has now hit our little St. Kitts
But instead of fighting back, people are playing politics.
The good doctors are warning us and trying to keep everybody sane,
Sadly, their reward includes the tarnishing of their good name.

For weeks upon weeks we have been forewarned,
But many still believed that the virus would soon be gone.
Quite a while now it's been lurking around our shores,
But now just a few weeks later it's right at our front doors.

The much larger countries are having a hard
time controlling this pandemic,
Yet some thought, that we were too special to get it.
Many are swarming the supermarkets even
if they're not sure of the reason,
Shopping up a storm like it's the start of the hurricane season.

When we were told to take great heed before this thing hits,
The doctor's opinion was almost literally, beaten with sticks.
Still they're out there, trying to do their best,
Advising us that part of the remedy, is to get enough rest.

As the news came out, that we have our first 2 cases,
One could now see the look of great fear, on many faces.
Scorning the victims, won't make you comfortable,
In fact, the next known case, could be sitting
right next to you, at your dinner table.

Now is not the time, to start spreading or believing rumors,
But instead, think of how you can protect you and yours.
Don't feel awful that we now have a ban on all flights,
Because we're dealing with something that won't go overnight.

Whether it came by boat, or by airplane,
It's not going to disappear, by tarnishing people's names.
So please be civilized, and get a hold of yourselves,
If it gets out of control, who can we blame, but ourselves.

One could talk and talk from now until forever,
But please let's join as one, like we do when there's stormy weather.
Then and only then, can we this problem try to fix,
And restore the good name and credibility of one
and all, in our beloved little St. Kitts.

ELECTIONS

It's that time once again which we call the silly season,
Where families, friends and even lovers, fall out for no apparent reason.
We say that we strongly, believe in democracy,
Yet because we voted opposite, you want to kill me.

C'mon my people we can do better than that,
It shouldn't matter who voted the hand and who the hat.
When will we get over, the petty party politics,
And make that choice, without trying to work tricks

After the election is all said and done,
The majority members will start making decisions,
They will have to come together and do what's best for our country,
But who will remove, the wedge driven between you and your family.

You see, old people say where things start ain't there they end,
A lot of whom will be enemies, once were best friends.
Some will go out in two's, and some in fives,
And if their party loses, they're ready to jeopardize their lives.

Vote on the issues, facts and also stats,
And not because your grandma says, if you vote
against my party, don't bother come back.
Then and only then, can we really see change,
Instead of for the next five years, we play the blame game.

It is our fundamental right, to vote for who we want,
Yet others just do it, for what they'll get after the big day is gone.
That right there is a recipe for disaster,
And oh, don't forget about that real thing called karma.

Once given the mandate, the winning candidates will move on,
But you didn't vote for them, so you say some cheating went on.
Then follows the foolish, vandalism and violence,
Next thing you know you're behind 1840's high fence.

It really matters, whether we voted or not,
But at the end of the day we're all that we've got.
So please think about our future generation,
And don't get caught up in the dirty part of elections.

EMPOWERING OUR WOMEN

Even though the Lord might have given man dominance over the house,
That doesn't say he should make the woman feel as small as a mouse,
The common goal should be the upkeep of the home,
It's very difficult when either one tries to do it alone.

Who makes the most money should not be a competition,
For that was not His idea of having dominion.
We always say that one hand cannot clap,
But if she gains a little more knowledge she's
sometimes greeted with a slap.

If she goes off to college and passes her subjects honestly,
All she asks in the world of work is to be treated fairly.
For no job was assigned to any specific gender,
Be it a big strong man, or a woman that is slender.

Trampling her with dirty words and neglect,
Will never, ever, get you any greater respect,
From either the small man, or the big bosses,
Because as you slip up, they too will cut their losses.

Things and times are changing all over the world as we can see,
So why shouldn't she do construction, but,
yet a male is the office secretary.
As problems arise, men sometimes run out of solutions,
Yet he feels ashamed, to hear a woman's opinion.

Nothing is wrong if you give a woman even a small chance,
For life is not measured by who wears the biggest pants.
It would make our life so much easier as men,
If we just willingly share the hard work with
the willing and able women.

Politics was thought, to be a man's job all along,
But just look at how Jacinth, Marcella and
Constance proved them all wrong.
You even think that a female DJ is like a big bag of jokes,
But we have one of the best in the world, our very
own Michelle 'Sweet Sister Sensia' Stokes.

So, gender equality doesn't need any more explanation,
Let's just be open minded and fully embrace our hard-working women,
For when you make excuses and say that her place is in the kitchen,
Can you do her greatest job, which is child bearing?

FIGHT AGAINST CORONA

Everyone was looking forward to this 2020,
But now, we have the worst pandemic of the century.
Forcing us to do things we never did before,
Sanitizing everything, even your feet before they touch the floor.

Physical and social distancing is what we now have to practice,
Unless you want to be, the latest statistic.
Are we really serious, about following guidelines?
Or are we going to just continue doing, what we do, all the time.

Wearing a mask is now the safest thing,
But some think it looks better, under their chin.
Rules are put in place, to protect all of us.
But when employees try sanitizing your hands, you then start to cuss.

Should we challenge everything, that's for our own good,
Having police chase people, in the neighborhood.
Ignoring the warnings, about staying inside,
Because it's more fun when sighted, to run duck and hide.

As it's said, time lost can never be gained,
So, it's no mystery, our lives will never ever be the same.
Forget about what you're accustomed to in the past,
And get with the new program if you want to last.

Many persons are trying to adhere, to the new normal,
Almost everything is now done via virtual.
It's no problem to join online dances and fetes,
But the church links haven't reached, one hundred views as yet.

Staying six feet apart, is proving to be very challenging,
Since we're a friendly nation, and always bonding.
That has to now, go on the back burner,
For the survival of our people, in the future.

We won't always like, decisions made by leaders,
But at the end of the day, do what's best to
protect your brothers and sisters.
Find some alone time and reevaluate yourself,
And decide if you prefer life, or a RIP picture, placed on a shelf.

FIGHT 'TIL YOU WIN

You've taken my relatives and close friends,
All I can do is wonder when will the taking of lives end.
You sneak into our bodies then start spreading wild,
We feel sorry for the adults but what about that unborn child.

It's hard to eat right when the proper foods are so expensive,
So, we must find another method to get on the defensive.
It's so much easier to buy the process foods,
And that's also the main difference between
a healthy and a slowly dying dude.

The poor can't afford to buy organic stuff,
It's very difficult when the cashier says, sorry
sir but you don't have enough.
So, all we can do is turn to what we can afford to buy,
Because when you get home, looking at you are 3 pairs of hungry eyes.

Whether we're extremely rich or we have just enough,
All of us will hear the words, ashes to ashes dust to dust.
Cancer and other diseases don't pick out where to strike
But concentrate on hurting adults, teens and babies alike.

It's important to serve God; and also, to pray,
But he also helps those who help themselves at the end of the day.
So, don't think, because you go to church every Sunday,
That you're excused from pain and dismay.

We need to go back to being our brother's keeper,
Sharing locally grown foods and drive out the dreadful cancer.
Selfishly holding back from others because you say you too have to live,
Won't make a difference when cancer strikes
because it only takes it doesn't give.

I long to see the days when we go back to caring for each other,
For then and only then can we win the fight together.
Exercise, eat right and get plenty rest,
For at the end of the day your body should be your greatest interest.

I write all these words not for riches or fame,
But am tired of seeing us carelessly lose lives again and again.
So please heed my words and try to do better,
So, we can try our best and finally eradicate cancer.

FREEDOM

F- Fabulous, even more fabulous than the fab 5,
Is just one of the many words associated with Freedom 106.5.
Fulfilling your every desire from dusk till dawn,
God bless the day this beautiful station was born.

R- Righteous in every way, we keep our attitudes,
Respecting everyone and not being rude,
Taking little effort in order to do that,
Positively moving forward and never looking back.

E- Entertainment, one of the many things that we provide,
Bring your ads to us and we'll air them with pride.
Do it yourself and put it in your own way,
Or check our Ad Specialists, Juni, Sugar Bowl, Sensia or EK,

E- Extra special effort we put out all the time,
And that makes our station truly one of a kind.
Leaving no room, for any negative vibes,
Don't you dare move that dial from 106.5.

D- Difference in radio broadcasting, is what we make,
Always keeping it real, no time for being fake.
Take some time, to come and meet us and you'll see,
That we're not lying when we say we have a closely-knit family.

O- Overlooking our nation by means of media broadcasting,
It's a very serious task that we take on each and every morning.
Never be anxious to just push the radio aside,
Because in order to keep up with latest news, let freedom be your guide.

M- Magnificent is this station and you can bet on that,
An overall well-rounded media house and that's a well-known fact.
Today is the day that Freedom FM turns nine,
And will only get better like the finest aged wine.

GOD IS IN OUR MIDST

When uncomfortable things happen to us, we never quite understand,
That the Lord is simply saying that it's His and not our plan.
We hustle and bustle and are always on the move,
But He sometimes uses sickness to show us we have nothing to prove.

I have a good friend, she goes by the name of **Melda Nolan**,
Whom right now, has limited use of both her hands.
But am sure no matter her ordeal, she's giving God praise,
We might not believe it but, He just might restore her to glory days.

So, whenever we feel, like God is against us,
Remember, it was always milk and honey,
before mankind betrayed His trust.
Causing the whole world, to run like a ship that's gone adrift.
But He's still the one true God, and will always be in our midst.

Most people only remember God when things don't go their way,
But when you are running around speeding, do you remember to pray?
Because if only when trouble arises you go on bended knees,
You'll be someone, in whom He's not pleased.

He allows us to have our own way, most of the time,
But just like humans, he also draws the line.
Still though, not leaving us on our own to suffer,
That's easy for Him to do as He is our father.

The Bible is fulfilling as told in days gone by,
We have to be more mindful of the lives we live, both you and I.
Not knowing when or what will be our faith,
Let's take stock of our lives before it's too late.

We can see it every day as we walk by and by,
Life is so amazing, just look at the birds that fly,
Just by one spread and a single flap of their wings,
They're off soaring high above, looking down on everything.

So whenever in doubt and not sure where to go,
Look to God as he's the same as he was
yesterday and will also be tomorrow.
And if you still ask questions about who He really is,
The same God who woke you this morning will always be in our midst.

GREEN VALLEY FES

Most of our communities, have their own adventure,
One of the greatest things we possess, which is our culture.
Not taking anything, away from any one of them,
But what we have here in Green Valley, truly is a gem.

At different times of the year we display our best,
By hosting what we call, our Village Fest.
Not for competing, against each other,
But instead, trying to push our country ahead, even further.

All the communities are stepping up their game,
By now we should all, know them by name.
Some are trying, to revive and renew their cultural spirit,
But here in Cayon, we always had, and still do have it.

The circus actors, who jump through hoops,
Still can't compare to our parade of folklore and troops.
Take it a little further for those who don't know,
And listen to our social commentary which we call calypso.

SP people does say, hub, hub, hub from dusk till dawn,
But in Green Valley we simply say, Cayon... Nobody On.
We had a Lotta pace when we were Cayon Sunquick.
But we're even faster now that we're **FLOW 4G Cayon Rockets**.

It's a grand occasion to see us playing mas,
Our village is not the biggest, but we not coming last.
Because other communities, in size might be greater,
But we're on a different level, when it comes to beauty and splendor.

Those who visit our fest, from far or near,
Are so amazed, that they now want to move here.
So that they can always have, an opportunity to see our culture,
It's now being said, they haven't seen one better.

We take much pride in our cultural aspect,
So much so, that we have earned our visitors respect.
Always taking our talent, to a very high level,
Am sure if you look closely, you'll find **Cayon
Green Valley Fes** in Google.

HAPPY BIRTHDAY BETHESDA

It's proven difficult nowadays, to get people into church,
All because most people, simply have the wrong approach,
We all have, our own philosophy,
Yet Jesus still loves us all unconditionally.

Whether you're from country or from town,
keep sending up the prayers, and the blessings will come down.
Flowing without cease front, back, center and right,
The result is the same, whether by day or night.

Sometimes your life might seem oh so bitter,
But there is such a place that can make u feel much better.
Am talking about, a feeling that lasts forever,
Given freely by the missionaries of Bethesda.

The whole Moravian conference, is truly blessed,
From the pastor, right down to the very smallest.
Each point of the building, forms a corner,
But the whole sanctuary is constantly blessed, by Rev Ervin Warner.

If you don't have a church home, you're welcome,
To join any one of the provinces of Moravian,
Having sanctuaries, in all corners of the earth,
Attend as an adult or from as early as child birth.

All of us have come together for one common cause,
To cherish life and our creator, almighty God.
It isn't a competition to see which church lasts long,
For if that was the case, we're doing good at 201.

WINGS OF HOPE

Walk for a cure, walk to save lives,
Today it's your neighbor's husband, tomorrow it may be your wife.
For by walking you've just made a good start,
To prolonging your most precious artery, which is your heart.

Don't be fooled it takes kids also,
Do regular check-ups and prevent unwanted sorrow.
Because, you can be, as strong as an ox or as fit as a fiddle,
None of us are too big or even too little.

We constantly hear the cry, his or her, death came as a shock,
Yet, still we find time for leisure dates and forget the one with our doc.
Only when cancer, comes knocking on our door,
Is when we find time to sit in his office for 2 hours or maybe even 4.

Most of the time, that dreadful sentence he has to give,
Ma'am it's now critical and you have but a few months to live.
Now men, don't think for one minute that we're out of the do,
Because we, can also get breast cancer too.

Cancer comes in all form, shape and size,
And doesn't leave until it claims at least one in every 3 lives.
Return the message and send it with all your might,
Let cancer know you've already started walking and dieting right.

Again, I say fight on we must,
Until the dreadful disease is left in our dust.
Then and only then can we emphatically say,
This is a cancer free body so you can just go away.

KEEP OUR COUNTRY CLEAN

The smell and look of your garbage makes you turn up your face,
Then you look at me and expect me to take it
up because I work for solid waste.
I have no problem because that's what am paid to do,
But keeping our country clean is the responsibility of both me and you.

Known to be one of the cleanest islands in the Caribbean,
Do whatever it takes and help us to continue this trend.
Go a little further and help accomplish our goal,
Of being the number one, cleanest country in the world.

Because we're highly dependent on the tourism industry,
Always think first of our beautiful country.
And play your part in keeping it clean,
So we can be featured, in top five tourist destination magazines.

It's not something very difficult to do,
Just think about cleanliness in everything that you do,
Soon you'll see how very easy it is,
Once everyone takes garbage disposal as a serious business.

Don't say, that it's the government's sole duty,
To preserve the cleanliness of this our beautiful country.
But instead, always be willing to do your part,
Because it's easy and doesn't need a special art.

Solid waste management corporation manages the final disposal,
But before that we all must properly bag and secure our refusal,
If this is done properly by both old and young,
We'll show up the other islands on how garbage disposal is done.

When visitors come to our town and visit the many beautiful scenes,
They're often amazed at how such a small island is kept so clean.
These praises should not go without mention,
Thanks to the early morning workers who
religiously make sure that it's done.

Apart from helping to promote that vital industry,
Helping to preserve healthy lives should be our sworn duty.
So the next time you feel the urge to go and litter,
Think of the serious consequences that follow right after.

KING SUGAR

Once again, we've reached another year,
And that guy called sugar is still bringing endless joy and cheer.
We all know that he's very passionate about birthdays,
Am sure right after his last one he began counting the days.

His phone will be flooded with messages in galore,
Bet you sweet dollar he going read all for sure.
So, don't fret and think that yours didn't matter,
He will acknowledge you even if it's later.

Every morning he religiously goes on the express,
Even when at times he isn't feeling the best.
We all love him even though some pretend to be angry,
When he talks during a song and they say, "bah de boy like talk see".

I think he got tired, and fed up of being chubby,
He's now training under his gym coach Cally.
Gone from wearing X-large tops and loose khaki,
To now fitting in some medium tight jerseys.

He loves a lot of cake and even more Vita malt,
But that won't put, his training at a halt.
Check him every afternoon running on the by-pass,
Doing his best to shed dat weight and don't come last.

He first tried the plaits which lasted kind of long,
After which he decided to join the Mohawk gang.
Then he went low cut for a couple of days,
And now found his place in de land of de fade.

Leslie, Rajaurn or Sugar, call him anyone,
But he only answers to all if you're a real fan.
So, don't get vex if you try it and don't get a response,
A warn you already and you do it more than once.

I can speak from now till the end of days trying to describe him,
But I can't seem to find much more words
than extraordinary and loving.
He's as good as a best friend can ever be to me,
But don't get it twisted a still calling him Leslie.

LET FREEDOM REIGN

The 30th of August some 8 years ago
Came into existence what we know as Freedom Radio
Though the journey might sometimes seem tiring and long
Just like the energizer bunny we're still going strong.

It's not a competition against the other stations,
But still feel free to tell us congratulations.
Because apart from being highly favored and blessed,
Duely informing the general public is what we do best.

As you wake in the morning and you're looking for motivation,
Just turn your dial to the morning inspiration.
There's always a blessing in some good gospel,
And that's exactly what you get from the man brother Bernel.

Right after him comes that guy Sugar Bowl,
Who is always hot and never gets cold.
You listen him and say your day he just made,
Don't say he talks too much because that's why he's being paid.

Tune in if you just simply want to hear the news,
Or leave that dial and join in the issues.
Express yourself but use clean words,
As there's a no-nonsense host in one Clement Junie Liburd.

Island rhythm takes you from afternoon into the evening,
With your sweet Frenchman who knows how to please your wanting.
He teaches and pleases and makes you want to say,
That none can compare to de sweetest Rasta man called EK.

The queen of radio now sits in the chair,
That's Sweet Sister Sensia who's always pushing local talent on the air.
She's like an angel sent down from heaven,
Who wants nothing more than to love and save our children.

It might be raining and you're feeling kinda cold,
Just listen to Julie Charles who'll soothe your mind, body and soul.
You can either sort yourself out inch by inch,
Or leave it up to that bald head guy from
Cayon called the one DJ Rinch.

Talk about a calypso and say it's from way back,
It doesn't matter because nobody knows that field like Lord Black.
There are others working behind the scene, who you might not know,
But this is one big happy family here at Freedom Radio.

Freedom is a well-rounded station that keeps your spirit alive,
Just in case you don't know the dial, it's 106.5.
And you've heard us all say again and again,
When it comes to media broadcasting **FREEDOM** will always reign.

LOVE THEM DON'T MISTREAT THEM

When God gave man dominion over this land,
Nowhere in the script did it say he should beat up on a woman.
You beat, rape and leave them to suffer,
But how would you feel if someone did the same thing to your sister.

You do the shameless deed then say your emotions ran wild,
Then right after, you claim you're sorry and
expect her to conceive your child.
She's so afraid of you that she does your request,
But right after giving birth, you beat her again
before the child even comes off her breast.

No matter your beliefs or types of religion,
It's a shameful and cowardly act when you beat up on a woman.
You say your neighbor is too nosey when they peep over your fence,
But that's just an excuse to continue the gender based violence.

What if that child is born a little girl,
And she falls victim, to other vicious men like you in this world.
Or what if it so happens that you get a son,
Would you train him to beat women if they
didn't agree with his opinion?

We cannot continue, to treat women like old rags,
Use and abuse them then dispose of them like a disposable bag.
Because, even though the higher ratio might be on their side,
If the violence continues you might not be able
to find a living one for your bride.

I know it's not easy when the women try to speak out,
Especially when the majority of blows suffered, caught you in the mouth.
But then again when the police try to take the culprit in the van,
You foolishly grab onto him and say you can't do without your man.

So, both genders have a lot of work to do,
Or else our unborn children will put their feet in the wrong shoe.
Then one ends up in the cemetery and the other a cell mate,
We need lots more love and finish away with the hate.

I am a man who respects any and every woman,
After all I wouldn't be here if it wasn't for one of them.
So I'm begging and pleading to all men no
matter the race, creed or nature,
Please let us truly love and enjoy, our greatest
gift given to us by our Creator.

MANGOLAND CAFÉ

It all started with a dream you scarcely spoke about,
But am sure when you did, Toni just screamed and shout.
You shared your ideas and she was oh so interested,
And you both never worried, about the money that had to be invested.

Like most businesses, you started out small,
Then in no time you barely had room for all.
And for you it was never about the money,
But pleasing the customers, with your charming personality.

Other big-name cafes might be dressed up and fancy,
That is OK, your simple but exquisite place makes customers happy.
You created your own original and unique look,
And make the fanciest delicacies, without looking in a book.

Now it's almost a year and things were going great,
Then came the sad news, that you will have to close your gates.
Am not even worried about what you will now do,
Because God always handles the tough decisions, for people like you.

Nothing can stop you from carrying on your dream,
Not even the dreaded and dangerous Covid19.
Because, in the midst of it all, you still kept your staff working,
And never eased up, on the utilities or rent paying.

You catered for everyone and never turned anyone away,
That's the perfect recipe, for a successful business today.
Some came for breakfast, and some for lunch,
There was also extra, for those who wanted brunch.

When your heart; and passion goes into something,
No man or woman alive, can stop those wheels from turning.
You, being a rare, kind-hearted individual,
Will just move on and will not take it personal.

You are blessed in so many ways, in this life,
One of your greatest, being Toni, your loving wife.
The man up above is looking down on this champion,
I didn't say it yet? Oh, his name is **Julian.**

MICHELLE

M - Mindful Mother, of the decisions she now makes in her life,
Because like everyone else, she too was not always this wise.
Living for the moment and just being a normal teenager,
But turned all that around, and made
preparations for her beautiful daughter.

I - Inspirational to more people, than what you can count,
Her life is measured not by who she helps, but the amount.
Notwithstanding that, she too also has her bills to pay,
That doesn't stop her from helping others day to day.

C - Caring for people's feelings, instead of what they say,
In spite of all the rumors she endured day after day.
They even said, her chances of child bearing were already too late,
God proved them all wrong and blessed her
with a bundle of joy called faith.

H - Honest with her inner feelings whether you like it or not,
At the end of the day it accounts for a lot.
Because no matter what you do people will always talk,
But the bigger person, is always the one who keeps silent and away walks.

E - Entertaining, whenever she goes on the DJ set,
Choose another female, and see you'll lose the bet.
Even against the guys, she pulls her own weight.
Whether she plays early or goes on the mic late.

L - Loveable person, once you take time to find out,
Instead of listening to rumors, as they know not what they speak about.
Yes, it's true, we all have our own mind,
That still doesn't change the fact that she's very kind.

L - Laughing always, she doesn't have time to get vex,
If you need advice and can't find her, just send a text.
Whatever you choose, you can be your own judge,
It doesn't make sense her reputation try to smudge.

E - Extraordinary as anyone can be,
She's a great friend, to both you and me.
So, come on and give to her, just what is due,
Because I know you would want the same if it were you.

By now I think, that the name should ring a bell,
We should all know, am talking about Michelle.
Yes, that same one who's always giving jokes,
That full eye girl from Market Street who
belong to Pam and Mickey Stokes.

MOTHER

M - Majestic she is, like an eagle soaring the sky,
That's a fact well known by both you and I.
Always soaring to new heights while on us looking down,
She has the same mentality, never forsaking her young.

O - Observant always about her near and far surroundings,
Every situation is given value, when others see them as nothing.
Analyzing very carefully what's going on,
If you're right she'll defend you but will also chastise you if you're wrong.

T - thankful to the lord for his love and tender mercy,
Counting all her blessings bestowed on her and her family.
Because she knows how important it is to give gratitude,
You'd better do the same or else you'll come as being rude.

H - Helpful in every possible way, one could think about,
Do what's expected and don't make her scream and shout,
Because as much as she loves you and is understanding,
Too much disobedience would be begging for a spanking.

E - Enthusiastic, and always looking for new avenues,
To ensure that in us she instills proper values.
Not just any old teaching, or improper ways,
But priceless values taught to her, in the good old days.

R - Respectful of every man, woman, boy or girl,
Quite obviously the most precious gem that we have in this world.
Never leaving any family member behind,
Truly all mothers are one of a kind.

Giving them all the love and respect that is due,
Don't be ashamed because she'll just give it right back to you.
We can stand today and proudly say as men,
God gave us the greatest gift and may he forever bless all women.

UNCLE/FATHER

There's a very big hearted, special man walking this earth,
Who always has, and still is always there for me, from since my birth.
I was very little, and people would always
laugh, when I said he was my father,
Because they all knew, he was my mother's brother.

He was the main male figure in my life, as I grew up,
Nurturing and caring for me, like a mother to her pup.
He didn't have to single me out and take me under his wings.
Because he saw, I was ready and willing, to do just about anything.

Whenever he gave me a chore it was quickly done,
And he also sometimes forgot, I was his nephew, and not his son.
We all knew the difference, but always thought it was funny,
That the bond we share is like a bee to its honey.

He never hesitates but always helps me out,
Even if I just made him scream and shout.
But that's something that rarely occurred,
Because just by the stern look, he didn't have to say a word.

He made sure I got the tools, to get a proper education,
And guaranteed that one day, I'd make a big change in our nation.
Everyone is now seeing that come to pass,
As we're both equal partners, in a tyre shop with plenty class.

I trained under him repairing tyres since the age of eight,
And was constantly reminded that one day, I'd be just as great.
By the age of 12 he started allowing me to run the business,
Which paved the way, for my now mentionable progress.

Being the best man at my wedding, was a hands down choice,
As I got from him an eternity of knowledge and advice,
Our bond will never need to be repaired,
Just to mention his name, made me go into tears.

It's so very easy, for me to write about my special uncle,
And not worry, about what to do,
In my opinion there's not another so admirable and just,
Than my forever loving uncle, Ronald Boy Blue Thomas.

C. A. R. L. T. O. N

C - Charismatic as one person could ever be,
Oh, you should have seen him when he was a referee.
When you thought you could play dirty and get away with it,
Out came his red card and back to the locker
rooms you'd have to go and sit.

A - Ambitious is his attitude from since he was small,
But he wasn't always successful and got a few falls.
Still that didn't stop him from pursuing his dream,
Of selling, repairing and always keeping your jewelry clean.

R - Resilient, in many ways and not just looking tough,
When he entered into politics, some called him bluff.
And though he did not win, in that very race,
He accepted his loss and moved on with grace.

L - Lustily are his words, can keep a good conversation,
But don't say the wrong thing or that soon will be done.
Because the more you talk, he'll just stand and stare,
Then move on from you, as if you weren't even there.

T - Trustworthy to the public, when conducting business,
While teaching you, about getting maximum profits.
Never selling you short, when you offer your gold,
Giving you the best offer whether you're young or old.

O - Overwhelming love is what he has to share,
Spreading it to the public, every morning on the air.
That's a big part, of his very existence,
Come get some, from the Dupont Experience.

N - Noble is the way, he defines his attitude,
Though some might disagree, and say he's being rude.
Stick to your opinion, and he to his also,
The only one who can change that, is his good friend Tango.

These traits are just a few, of this Sandy Point man,
Who's always ready and willing, to lend a helping hand.
By now it's obvious, who's story am on,
The one and only, Carlton, Emmanuel, Rastafari without locks Dupont.

OUR CULTURE

Each island has their own adventure,
And our greatest one, is our culture.
Not taking anything from any one of them,
But what we have here, truly is a gem.

At different times of the year we display our best,
When some of the communities, host their village fest.
Not for competing, against each other,
But instead, trying to push our country ahead further.

All the areas have stepped up their game to a higher level,
Don't say which one is better or you might get into trouble.
SP say hub-hub, and go on and on,
But in d green valley we say, Cayon...nobody on.

The circus actors, who jump through flaming hoops,
Still can't compare, to our grand parade of troops.
Take it a little further for those who don't know,
And listen to our social commentry which we call calypso.

It's a grand occasion to see us playing mas,
Our country might be a little small but we not coming last.
Because other islands in size might be greater,
But we're on a different level when it comes to beauty and splendor.

Those who visit our country from far or near,
Are so amazed, that they try to purchase land or property here.
To have an opportunity to always see our culture,
They're all saying, they haven't seen one better.

We take much pride, in our cultural aspect,
So much so, that we have earned our visitors respect.
Always taking it, to a very high level,
Am sure if you look good, you'll find us on Google.

Try our tasty local food which is sure to fill your tummy,
Then get on the route, and have a good look at the moko-jumbie.
Never ever settling, for less than the best.
Visit us in June and take a look at the region's greatest music fes.

We have so much to offer, and plenty to share.
Visit our sister island Nevis, and you'll find the same there,
Foreigners always come back, from time to time,
To experience the one and only, greatest summer lime.

Am talking about, what we call culturama,
Endless food, fun, pageantry and folklore.
I think by now we can all safely say this,
There ain't no other twin island federation like St. Kitts and Nevis.

BLESSINGS COME
IN MANY WAYS

Right now you think, that your life is very rough,
Barely finding food, and even when you do, it is not enough.
But it's not just about you alone anymore,
Instead, you've got a family of four.

You sometimes wonder, what will they eat today,
But the good lord helps you, to get them fed and on their way.
It's not a shame, when you have life real hard,
And I know you do what you can, in that regard.

Your dwelling place, might have been old and shabby,
And no proper place, to raise a family.
Still, you made sure to press on every day,
Until a helping hand, came along the way.

Blessings can flow, in more ways than one,
Especially, when you think that your life is over and done.
Because the lord knows, just how much we can bare,
And steps right in and removes all our fear.

The most important thing, is to keep God as head of the house,
Because he cares for all, right down to a very little mouse.
Let that be your guide, as you go along your way,
Knowing that, he will be right by your side every day.

There might have been times, when you cried in silence,
And other times you let it out, in your kids presence.
All because you know that you were trying your best,
And now you're seeing that this family is truly blessed.

Just when you thought, you've reached the end of your rope,
Outstretched hands came along, and gave you hope.
For this I know, you'll be forever thankful,
And continue living a life, now very fruitful.

This blessed family, will now move forward in the world,
And live an ordinary life, like any other boy and girl.
But of course, not forgetting where we came from,
We'll always praise God, whose will is being done.

APPRECIATE LIFE

To wake up each day, should be considered a blessing,
Because someone out there, didn't make it through the evening.
Life can be beautiful filled with joy and laughter,
But you have to first know, what it is you're really after.

We were all made in the likeness of God,
But only appreciate each other, when we go abroad.
Don't forsake, what you have here at home,
As the TV paints a good picture but hundreds live alone.

BULLYING DOESN'T PAY

It's always easy to beat up on a lesser someone,
But what about when the fight changes position.
You beat up on your prey while others cheer with laughter,
Then as you wink the same thing happened to your sister.

You're now in a rage and your temper begins to swell,
Give in to this and you just might end up in a cell.
All in all, am just trying to say,
Bullying others has a terrible price to pay.

GOD'S STILL THERE

Just when we think, that we can do it on our own
In steps God to remind us, that He's still on the throne.
Over and over we fall short and lose our way,
And often times it's peer pressure, making us do wrong every day.

Don't say it's Satan, and start getting a fit,
But know that God brought you there, and He'll get you through it.
So, if for some strange reason you've lost your way,
Don't be afraid to look to God, he'll accept you today.

KNOW YOUR WORTH

If we're all created in our own unique way,
Then why wish you were, like that person you saw today.
Things might look, all good and well on the outside,
But they might just be, burning with pain on the inside.

So, whenever you get that feeling, just look around,
And tell yourself, you're already wearing a crown.
Because whether you were born as a king or a queen,
Your best treasure, is great self-esteem.

FRUITS OF THE SPIRIT

It's one thing to believe in the fruit of the Spirit,
But you should have peace within and not just when you read it.
For there is no greater joy, than real faith and true love,
Not just for earthly beings, but also for our Father above

Jesus endured, much pain and long-suffering,
All because He's a meek and gentle being.
Having all of us as his greatest interest,
He meant it when he said he was giving us all his mercy and goodness.

A DECADE OF FREEDOM

They say time flies when you're having fun,
And so it continues when you listen to freedom.
We captivate an overwhelming audience all over,
who can't get enough of our programs and music of all genres.

Very keenly listening, to each and every word said,
from since brother Bernel wakes them up, till
when DJRinch puts them to bed.
Choose your time of day, when you want to tune in,
Have an early morning laugh, or some midday easy listening.

When you talk about broadcasting, at its very best,
don't blame us, if we're a cut above the rest.
Doing what we love to do each and every day,
we don't always feel like it, but we do it anyway.

A line for local callers and one for overseas,
John also got the Wallers involved, with such ease.
Reaching as much people as possible, is the main aim,
so modern technology was introduced, to step up our game.

We're on a progressive path, not looking back,
and can't be stopped, just like Kim Collins on the track.
Putting our best foot forward, to keep ahead of the race,
Always Fresh ideas, keep us moving at a very fast pace.

We all make choices about how we choose to live,
Same goes for which station we listen, but be
careful, freedom is very addictive.
The critics all said, that we wouldn't last,
But hey check your calendar, a decade has just passed.

Thank God for Juni and the decision he made 10 years ago,
And by his blessings we will be here to serve
you every day and tomorrow.
Your active participation is what keeps us going,
And the love you the fans show us, is never ending.

Jester, Jihan, Jaimie, brother Bernel and DJ Right Hand,
DJ Flames, Clivette, DJ Rinch, and Webmaster John,
EK, Sensia, Sugar Bowl and Juni Liburd,
The world class family, from the world class station,
thanking God for a decade of love.

A REAL MAN – A REAL FATHER

From the tender stage of a baby, children mostly cling to their mothers,
But there wouldn't even be a fetus without the help of a father.
He plays a major part in the upbringing of children
That they won't soon forget even if he has died and gone to heaven.

A real father leaves his family wanting for nothing,
And with God's help, he's their rock and their everything.
Whatever there is around the house to be done,
Do it or else when dinner is cooked you won't be getting none.

He is supposed to show his family love and respect,
But it's sad when sometimes the only thing shown is neglect.
Children need a role model and someone to look up to,
Start doing this early; even help them to tie the laces of their shoes.

Some say more attention should be paid to the boys,
But he better don't even think about that
when it comes to buying their toys.
Because children as well as wives or girlfriends
look forward to their gifts.
Do not you dare forget a special occasion or you'll
be outside with your clothes begging a lift.

Everything in life has its good and it's bad,
And the same goes to show for some of the so-called dads.
Who leaves their children and responsibilities behind.
But later on in life are the first to say, see the state
scholar on the far right, yes, he's mine.

Beating a child senseless doesn't do any good,
But instead, only drives them to look for love in the hood.
So have a kind, but stern word with them today,
And from your proper teaching they will never stray.

He gives his whole family equal and undying love,
After all that's what he was taught from our father up above.
Never forsaking or leaving anyone behind,
He is always there, just in the nick of time.

Imagine the look on a child's face when placed in a candy land,
The same goes for a woman when she realizes she's got a good man.
So please don't go around blaming all men,
because it seems you made a bad choice,
But instead, for Father's Day surprise him with a Rolls Royce.

Romaine Belgrove
18th June 2016

BLACK HISTORY

Many years ago, black men and women were bought and sold,
to their so called masters, who paid but a mere tiny piece of gold.
At that time, there was a lot of racial discrimination,
and putting up resistance, only ended up in one's elimination.

The strong black men were put in the fields, from dawn till dusk,
and couldn't utter a word, for this was a must.
The women on the other hand, even though in it they took no pleasure,
Had to fulfill, their master's every desire.

As long as your skin was black, you were considered minority,
and even if you were 100 % right, the upper
class was still given authority.
So the role of the men was to work until the end of their days,
and the women on the other hand just produced more baby slaves.

To move from the fields to the house, was a great accomplishment,
But disobey once, and you were right back on punishment.
The coloreds as they were called had to stay in their quarters,
without lights, beds, and even clean drinking water.

As the sun shone down and from a black strong body, sweat would drip,
the upper class women found this enticing, and lustily licked their lips.
Sooner or later, they would always have their own way with that man,
then along came a baby, with a naturally brown tan.

This of course, was not acceptable to Massa,
because in no way, shape or form, should a
black man sleep with his daughter.
And even though the black man did not pursue this upper class woman,
He was beaten severely, with whips and batons.

But thank God, along came the cavalry,
of brave men and women, who won the fight for you and me.
They gave it their all, whether in the light or in the dark,
People like Malcolm X, Martin Luther King and Rosa Park.

So when you look at me, and say that am colored,
we might have different pigmentation, but the same color blood.
And even though your hair is long and straight,
and mines short and nappy,
just remember, we're all part of God's loving family.

Romaine Belgrove
18/2/2017

CLEMENT JUNIE LIBURD.

Eight years ago, it started with a vision,
Now today in SK you have the best radio station.
Making a big difference in all of our lives,
You're the genius behind freedom FM 106.5

The good things about our community scarcely get said,
But you constantly remind us that you're Mc. Knight born and bred.
And in-spite of all the gang wars and violence going on,
You're never ashamed to tell us where you were born.

You were created by God and then groomed into a great man,
I think we can all say thank God for a mother like Anne.
She trained you to always be respectful and neat,
There's no secret her very existence was your heartbeat.

To talk about children that's even better,
Look at how you passed on your radio skills to DJ right hand and jester.
Constantly reminding us of the love for all your children,
Grading a good father, you'll get ten out of ten.

You're a good man with nuff roots and culture,
It doesn't have to be biological but every man is your brother.
And just like a scientist is very serious with his science,
You're the same with your race that's why you
started The Great Black Experience.

You've taken care of the body that was given to you by the almighty,
Many people out there can't believe that you're now 70
Sticking to natural herbs and all good things from the earth,
Never ever straying from the things taught to you from birth.

When you talk about respect he has that in abundance,
Every conversation with him always has good substance.
If you don't believe me just listen to the talk show issues,
No matter your status you still get a chance to air your views.

All in all, this great man is a son of our soil,
Don't think he had life easy because he already did his share of the toil.
And instead of waiting till they're gone like most people usually do,
Let's honor **CLEMENT JUNIE LIBURD** now while it's due.

Romaine Belgrove
3rd January 2019

DON'T LOOK BACK!!!!

Don't look back, on the year that has now gone by,
No matter what you do, the time will still fly.
You see, time lost can never be gained,
Whether it gave you joy, or caused severe pain.

Don't look back, and be upset about COVID-19,
Diseases have been around, since we were all teens.
Embrace the change instead, and all that it has taught us,
Since we were living our lives, like a runaway speeding bus.

Don't look back, feeling so sorry for yourself,
Just take back up that positive attitude, from off the shelf.
And try to live life, the way God meant it to be,
Accepting always, the good, the bad and the ugly.

Don't look back, carrying a bag full of regrets,
Shouldn't you be living, your best life yet?
Learning to forgive, all who might have done you wrong,
And not holding on every year, to the same old sad song.

Don't look back, storing built up anger,
When the thermometer hits red, it's unwanted danger.
Treat all others, the same way you know you should,
Evil begets evil, but could never outlast good.

Don't look back, and cry senselessly over all the deaths,
God is fulfilling his plan, and he's not finished yet.
So let go of the saying... Someone died before their time,
We all have a time clock, but I don't know
yours and you don't know mine.

Don't look back, blaming worldwide leaders for all that's going wrong,
We're in the game of life, just tagging along.
So don't think you can dictate, what will happen next,
Even the best gambler,
From time to time, loses a bet.

Don't, and never ever look back, wishing you had someone else's life,
What might seem rosy to you, could be
overwhelmed with pain and strife.
Always look forward, making the sky the limit for you and me,
God has taught us a lot, so let's just embrace all that happened, in 2020.

Romaine Belgrove
28/12/2020

FREEDOM 106.5

F- Fabulous, even more fabulous than the fab 5,
Is just one of the many words associated with Freedom 106.5.
Fulfilling your every desire from dusk till dawn,
God bless the day this beautiful station was born.

R- Righteous in every way, we keep our attitudes,
Respecting everyone and not being rude,
Taking little effort in order to do that,
Positively moving forward, and never looking back.

E- Entertainment, one of the many things that we provide,
Bring your ads to us, and we'll air them with pride.
Do it yourself and put it in your own way,
Or check our Ad Specialists, Juni, Sugar Bowl, Sensia or EK,

E- Extra special effort we put out all the time,
And that makes our station truly one of a kind.
Leaving no room, for any negative vibes,
Don't you dare move that dial, from 106.5.

D- Difference in radio broadcasting, is what we make,
Always keeping it real, no time for being fake.
Take some time, to come and meet us and you'll see,
That we're not lying when we say, we have a closely-knit family.

O- Overlooking our nation by means of media broadcasting,
It's a very serious task that we take on each and every morning.
Never be anxious to just push the radio aside,
Because in order to keep up with latest news, let freedom be your guide.

M- Magnificent is this station and you can bet on that,
An overall well-rounded media house, and that's a well-known fact.
Today is the day that Freedom FM turns nine,
And will only get better like the finest aged wine.

Romaine Belgrove
30/08/2019

G. E. O. R. G. E

G - Generous as any one person could ever be,
Always willing to share, with you and me.
And not just the physical things that one can give,
But also, his personal wealth of knowledge.

E - Enthusiastic, when it comes to sports,
Following closely, from the cricket pitch, to the tennis court.
You watched the game, but did not stay for the ending,
Do not worry, just ask and he will tell you who win.

O - Observant of not only his country, but the whole world,
Asking him for an update is like Pele scoring a goal.
Always precise and accurate too,
You still went to research and found out it is true.

R - Religious lifestyle, is what he's living up to this very day,
If you don't believe me, listen to morning
inspiration when he starts to pray.
Doing his best, to provide positive messages to our nation,
And leaves you wanting for more, even at the end of his session.

G - Grateful and thankful, that he's alive and well today,
Because this could have been an R. I. P
celebration, instead of happy birthday.
It is not easy losing a limb, and now considered differently able,
But his strong personality, is keeping him very nimble.

E - Extravagant and elegant, in conducting his affairs,
Just look at how he has his audience, dressed
so lovely sitting in those chairs.
Dress as good as u like and wear what you may,
Still, don't think for one minute, you're going
to outdo him on his special day.

We are all here, for one common, special cause,
So, rise from your seats, and give him a round of applause.
Lots of drinks here, and the food is plenty,
Give it up now, for **George Brother Bernel
Nolland**, who just turned the big 60.

Romaine Belgrove
19/12/2020

GOD BLESS ALL MOTHERS

We all look forward every year to the 2nd Sunday in May
for what is traditionally known as the official Mother's Day
I have searched and searched and are yet to find
enough gifts to repay you for being so loving and kind

Being a good mother is a very special art
you have to be willing to reason before you unleash your wrath
whether you're a biological, caretaker or guardian
all mothers are truly blessed in my humble opinion

You do what you do without want for attention
and it does not even bother you if your name is not mentioned
Seems you have been this way from since you were born
never being the one who toots their own horn

Every day other people get rewarded and praised
but you seldom get appreciation for your tireless nights and days
you never get any medals nor any trophy
and still your job you continue to do daily

Others are paid whenever they do work
Yet sometimes we seemingly forget your real worth
I want to give you your flowers while you're alive
Because once the queen bee leaves it's time for a new hive

When we don't get our own way, we sometimes get upset with you
but when trouble arises, you're the first one we run to
and because it's in your nature you outstretch your hand
Oh thank god mothers were part of the master plan

Man was made first we know that this is true
But the continuation of our species would be impossible without you
Fathers are also important in the raising of a child
Still a mother's love is always gentle, meek, and mild

So, it's about time you're given more than just one day
After all you always show endless love and affection in every way
am speaking to everyone and I hope you'll all hear
we need to make that change to **HAPPY MOTHERS YEAR!!**

Romaine Belgrove
09/05/2018

HARVEST

When you hear the word harvest, I bet you think about food,
But really it's the blessings laid upon us, whether you're a girl or a dude.
For you can be blessed in many ways, shape or form,
one may grow into it, or have it from the time you were born.

Harvest as we know, is reaping what we sow,
so make sure that your children, on the
straight and narrow path they go.
Teach and nurture them, in the way they should live,
be less quick to receive, and always eager to give.

Don't be like the servant, whom his talents he tried to hide,
But instead bless someone else, and by the lord's word you did abide.
Because if your taking over your giving, is much greater,
you just might soon be paid a visit, by the undertaker.

Be you a supervisor, CEO, or partner in a successful firm,
don't ever forget, you didn't get there on your own.
Just how the lord has blessed you, with more than enough to give,
remember there's others, depending on a scraping in order to live.

If farming is your passion, then go ahead and till the soil,
but whenever you reap, don't keep excess, until they begin to spoil.
Sometimes you might look up and wonder why,
there's no rain coming from the sky.
Just know that every disappointment is a blessing in disguise.

Learning to appreciate what you have, and always ready to give,
Will keep you in the lord's good grace, as long as you may live.
So harvest what you have sown, and do it with much pride,
because an honest day's work, will keep you by the lord's side.

Look all around you, and enjoy the fruits of
your brother's and sister's labor,
knowing that it all started, by trusting the lord as your savior.
From coconuts, or potatoes, to our bananas which we call fig,
whether they were grown on top or into the soil you had to dig.

Now go out into the world, and continue sowing good seeds,
because there's never any punishment for doing a good deed.
Sow your crops with passion, and be reminded every time that you do.
If you keep on trusting the lord, he will always continue to bless you.

Romaine Belgrove
22/10/2017

H. I. L. T. O. N

H - Honorable, from the crown of his head, to the soul of his feet,
in spite all the sayings about pork; it's still his favorite meat.
Talk to him, about anything in confidence,
and never worry about it reaching over your neighbor's fence.

I - Inspirational, in every possible way you could think of,
Knowledge is passed on to him from God, and it's always enough.
He will pass it on to you, totally free of cost,
Get it while you can, or it will be your loss.

L - Loyal, always to God, in carrying out his plan,
of saving as many souls, children, man or woman.
It's a tough battle, but he will never give up or give in,
this is one war, Satan you will never win.

T - Transparent, as if looking straight through, a freshly cleaned glass,
scarcely gets upset, and always a laugh.
Not putting his personal business, out there on the line,
but have a conversation, and know about him, all in time.

O - Outspoken, what you see, is what you get,
He's not going to butter up anything, or hold it till death.
Never been afraid, when time arises to put the fire under your feet,
Be it a politician, or the ordinary man on the street.

N - Necessary, in this world, is his humble life,
The Lord saw it fit, and blessed him with an even more peaceful wife.
We all know, that nobody is perfect,
But this example of a great marriage, is oh so correct.

Your transition came, with you not knowing what to expect,
but as loyal Moravians, we gave you our utmost respect.
And you transformed our sanctuary, into a one of a kind,
even after you leave, you'll always be on our mind.

You came to us willingly, and we had a very good run,
and if we had our own way, we'd tell the PEC, you now belong to Zion.
So for now we'll let go of the but, maybe and what ifs,
and share a little sample, of our blessed **Rev. Hilton J Joseph**.

Romaine Belgrove
28/12/2020

HOPE

Walk for a cure, walk to save lives,
Today it's your neighbor's husband, tomorrow it may be your wife.
For by walking you've just made a good start,
To prolonging your most precious artery, which is your heart.

Don't be fooled, it takes kids also,
Do regular check-ups and prevent unwanted sorrow.
Because, you can be as strong as an ox or as fit as a fiddle,
None of us are too big or even too little.

We constantly hear the cry, his or her, death came as a shock,
Yet, still we find time for leisure dates and forget the one with our doc.
Only when cancer, comes knocking on our door,
Is when we find time to sit in his office, for 2 hours or maybe even 4.

Most of the time, that dreadful sentence he has to give,
Ma'am it's now critical and you have but a few months to live.
Now men, don't think for one minute that we're out of the do,
Because we, can also get breast cancer too.

Cancer comes in all form, shape and size,
And doesn't leave until it claims at least one in every 3 lives.
Return the message and send it with all your might,
Let cancer know you've already started walking and dieting right.

Again, I say fight on we must,
Until the dreadful disease is left in our dust.
Then and only then can we emphatically say,
This is a cancer free body so you can just go away.

Romaine Belgrove
13/10/2018

HOPE, REACH, LIVE ON

When will a cure be found, for the dreaded disease called cancer,
Unfortunately, no one seems to have the answer.
Although that, should not be your question every morning,
But instead, what are you doing, to keep on living.

It's not something associated, only with the elderly,
Because today or tomorrow, it could be just about anybody.
So don't say, it won't affect you because you're still young,
As in the blink of an eye, your life on this earth could be done.

It's been known to affect, many females,
But don't even think about, excluding the males.
Because when we hear about breast cancer,
our first thought is always women,
We are oh so wrong, as this type also kills men.

The dominant killer of men is cancer in the prostate,
Though, most men are to blame for sealing their faith.
A lot of males are too proud to go see a doctor,
By the time they do, it's just a matter of time before they're done for.

It's already hard enough, that we have to deal with cancer,
And now came along, the dreaded COVID-19 or Corona.
We still can't just focus on what is now here,
But keep in mind what has been plaguing us year after year.

Be it cervical, lung, prostate or breast,
In the fight against cancer, we have to do our best.
Don't throw your hands in the air, and say your life is done,
Because it's as if you're saying, cancer has already won.

Many survivors often share their story,
And may the lord bless those, who have passed on to glory.
Leaving behind a known, and great legacy,
Hoping that the same thing, doesn't haunt
another member in their family.

We all need to know that there is still hope,
Even when we think, we're at the very end of the rope.
Fight for your friend, fight for your life and your dear family,
And always believe anything is possible, when you Reach For Recovery.

Romaine Belgrove
13/09/2020

JASON AMORY

The world of fashion is a very tough world to live in,
but when you're committed to such, to you it comes like nothing.
You give up your time and other things of interest,
Just to make sure that your models put out their best.

Many might not understand you and say you're a bit harsh,
but at the end of the day, you're softer than spray starch.
The models sometimes, break under pressure
and say they're going to quit,
but truth and in fact, they've already made
up their mind to put up with it.

All of your shows are not just about walking down runways,
but you always put a twist on them, after which
the audience always gives you your praise.
It takes a lot of time and certainly a lot more energy,
to pull off such a show, that's the talk of the whole country.

Whenever you come out you always put your best foot forward,
you sometimes make the models tremble, some
might even be considered coward.

With all that said and done I can say genuinely,
that when it comes to pulling off a proper show, there's
no other like Mr. Jason Stephen Amory.

Romaine Belgrove
22/10/2016

JILLIAN ARCHIBALD

J - Joyful is this woman, though most times mistaken,
Because of her robust attitude when giving her opinion.
When she gives you that look, it's not to scare you,
Because everything you hear is not always true.

I - Interesting and thought provoking, are her conversations,
Bring your A game, or you'll be seen as just an illusion.
She can keep it simple, or take it up a notch,
If you try to get technical, she'll show you what she got.

L - Loyal to her family, especially her children,
Talk all you may, but don't hit any of them.
I don't know, if she got it from her mother,
But when aggravated, she brings out the Newtown girl warrior.

L - Loveable as anybody, you'll find in this world,
And not just lately, but since she was a little girl.
Has a positive attitude, all day long,
Adhere to her teaching, and you can't go wrong.

I - Inspiring to all the young ladies, whom she taught,
That netball is about skill and not who's tall or short.
Her team ran through opponents, barely suffering any loss,
She's the nicest lady on the streets, but on the court, she's was very cross.

A - Ambitious and articulate, in every possible way,
Are just a few of her attributes, seen day to day.
There are so many things to say, I could write a story,
But for now, I'll just boast about that sweet tasting mauby.

N - No nonsense, is something she firmly stands for,
Don't mistake her sternness, for a bad temper.
You always hear, a dog's bite is worse than its bark,
But she was a force to be reckoned with, in Warner Park.

UWI certified, played locally, regionally
and overcame attempted knocks,
A proud founding member of the coca cola shamrocks.
A team that only knew how to win again and again,
Miss Jillian D.Archibald, you're now three scores and ten.

Romaine Belgrove
1/5/2020

JUST DANCE

Some people dance with a passion, some just dance for fun,
But whatever your reason, a real dancer doesn't
know the meaning of boredom.
You never need to be in the mood, to get up and dance,
All you have to do is move your feet and give it a chance.

Soon you'll find out that you're on the way,
To learning basic steps and not just the left to right sway.
Some types of dances also need special songs,
But it doesn't really matter so you can just tag along.

When the young at heart says, show me what you got,
The more mature minded just eases into a fox trot.
Question is then asked, what are you doing Mister?
Oh, I'm sorry son, we've moved on to the Bolero.

Any type of dance can be done to any kind of music,
All you have to do, is control your feet and put a little hip action into it
You don't know what you're doing, he says then laughs ha-ha,
That's quite alright my boy, but I bet you can't do the Cha Cha.

Practice by yourself, with a partner or in a ring,
Just as long as you're careful, and don't mess up the waltz timing.
Slow, medium, or the ticklish Viennese,
All look good, but make sure you have strong knees.

Salsa or meringue are used to impress,
The guy in the tuxedo or that beautiful lady in the short red dress.
Special steps are required, so take heed before you get up,
Remember you're doing a classy dance and not just the usual wuk up.

Stop saying to yourself that you don't know how to dance,
It's a form of exercise and also plays a big part in romance.
Yes, dancing is more than just going on the floor,
You and your partner have to be in sync to get a high score.

Dancing is a tradition, that we're hoping would live on,
Be it late in the evening, or at the break of dawn.
So, dance on my people and make it a day to remember,
When you came and saw this production by the St. Kitts Dance Theater.

Romaine Belgrove
29/11/2018

KIMBERLY 'LIL KYM' WARD

I first knew you, by seeing you in school many years ago,
Never knowing that we would be related sooner than tomorrow,
Whether it be, by blood or by law,
A pretty young lady with a bright smile is all I ever saw.

One of my fondest memories that I can't soon forget,
Is when you drove us across the Florida highway, like a runaway jet.
The tires on the vehicle were smooth and almost shredded,
When you touched that accelerator pedal, my
God, I thought we were all dead.

But being the carefree, thrill seeker whether near or far,
You just looked at us and said, "Hey it's not my car".
At first, we all thought, this girl must be crazy,
But then again, we knew you'd never try to
hurt your family intentionally.

A famous event was brought to Nevis a couple of years ago,
And who never knew you before, by now they all know.
We Caribbean people know how to do our thing,
You surely lived up, to the nick name 'Lil Kym'.

From the time you took that stage, we knew it was on,
Many were left in shock, especially Wyclef Jean.
We all looked and listened as you so well sang the part,
That many thought, could only be done by his female counterpart.

Singing was just, one of your additional attributes,
And you were well loved by both adults and youths.
You made some decisions, that would sometimes make one yell,
But at the end of it all, we knew you only meant well.

At a tender age, your passion for cosmetology woke up,
And you were soon widely sought by many,
to do their nails and makeup.
Your work was as flawless, as the feathers on a snow-white dove,
You did it to your best as this was your real true love.

Whenever we lose a loved one, sometimes we too feel like we want to die,
And we hope that you're looking down on us,
from that great big house in the sky.
Sipping milk and having conversations with God,
You'll forever be missed, KIMBERLY, 'LIL
KYM', 'SASHE MAC' WARD!!!

Romaine Belgrove
17/06/2019

LINCOLN

L - Lively a spirit as you'll ever find one to be,
and always a shoulder to lean on for both you and me.
If you need one he'll gladly lend a listening ear,
or just say the word and he'll be right there.

I - Industrious, and never being someone to waste time,
And when necessary, is able to relax and unwind.
Because of course he's also human you see,
and yes, he needs to make time for his family.

N - Noble as any one person can ever be,
Have a conversation with him, and you'll soon see.
That all he does is put others first,
and it's a blessing from God, and not a curse.

C - Caring, with a very, very, positive attitude,
always willing to help, and never being rude.
Will go all out for you and still add an extra mile,
He'll also captivate your heart, with that big broad smile.

O - Observant about his surroundings and also his actions,
dedicated a big part of his life, towards sanitation.
Moved on somewhat but still does it to an extent,
Call upon his company to get rid of the flies, ants or rodents.

L - Limitless when it comes to his time to praise God
doesn't really matter, if he's here at home, or abroad.
You might not believe in God, or even any religion,
He won't hold that against you as he respects everyone's opinion.

N - Necessary is this great man, in our world today,
and I think you'll all agree with me when I say.
We can't find enough words to add to his label,
yes, he's your friend, family and pastor, Lincoln........ Hazel.

MY BEAUTIFUL WIFE

It's been about 12 years since we first met if you're taking notes,
who knew that today, we'd be wondering if marriage could work.
I've been around the world and back and there
are many beautiful things to see,
but I think that the most beautiful, is standing right next to me.

Facial and bodily features are just an outer body look,
but to describe your inner beauty, I'd have to write a book.
You have so many good qualities I wouldn't even know where to start;
I think that's the whole reason why you stole my heart.

You are very independent and scarcely depend on anyone,
Sagittarius is your sign and you are a real champion.
You are very much admired by many others,
but only those who really know you will give you your flowers.

Whenever I'm around you I feel so alive,
especially when you smile and stare at me
with those beautiful bright eyes.
I wait patiently for your working day to be done,
because when you get home that's when our fun time has begun.

Romaine Belgrove
05/08/2016

PAMELLA

P - Passionate, with every last breath in her body,
Shows love to everyone and not just her family.
Every conversation with her, is worth your while,
But it's easy to get distracted, by that beautiful smile.

A - Astonishing, the way she does her work for so many years,
But she's also human and has shed her share tears.
Still proving that joy always cometh in the morning,
A prayer warrior who's always praying

M - Majestic like the feathers of a peacock,
You rock any fashion, whether skirt and blouse, or a simple frock.
Am sure, you've been doing that from since birth,
Your parents did a good job, teaching you your worth.

E - Extraordinary also, the way you raised Michelle,
No one can boast about a mother's love, quite as well.
Am sure she's passing on your words, to her daughter Chris,
No matter what they do to you, kill them with kindness.

L - Loyal to the love of your life, for so very long,
No matter who started it, or who's right or wrong.
Mickey Stokes am sure, is proud of his choice,
Since relationships today, are like rolling a dice.

L - Luxurious when you step out, but in a simple way,
Flawless victory is all they can say.
Even when the haters look at your life, and start gossiping,
Your kind heart still treats them like a human being.

A– Amazing, can't describe the size of your heart,
Always reserving a space, for your Sis Melda to play her part
It's just who you are, and no one can take that from you,
The world does not have enough feet, to fit in your shoe.

So now it's time, to celebrate your special day,
Gifts are all good, but not better than family me say.
You're surrounded by people who love you, now and forever,
Have a blessed birthday, my friend, **Pamella**.

Romaine Belgrove
4/5/2020

RAHEEM 'PIPE' FRANCIS

Positive and humble in every possible way,
Also one of the most confident, I must say.
This young man has certainly made his mark,
You can see it, every time he
plays football in the park.

If you don't really know him you might say he's boasting,
But that's just merely, his confidence building.
Always working hard at whatever he does,
What else can you do but just show him some love.

Most people think that an only child is easy to spoil,
But from small days his mother always taught him how to toil.
Don't look from the outside and try to judge her,
Just appreciate that she's just trying to be a good mother.

His team mates know that they can always count on him,
When a striker squeezes through, his chances of scoring are very slim.
One of the best defenders I have seen in a long time,
Friends on the road but on the field he draws the line.

A very well rounded player if I have ever seen one,
Cool, calm and collective when it's all said and done.
Very, very firm when he's defending at the back,
But also confident when joining in the attack.

He's a natural defender, by way of his position,
But can maneuver his way around the field when it has to be done.
If you make the mistake and let him score a goal,
You'll get a celebration that has never been seen or told.

Even in his unfortunate circumstances he manages to smile,
to bear so much pain and still in high spirits
you got to be a God blessed child.
Never known to be the one to start a fight,
He just looks at his mother and tells her he's going to be alright.

This young man has taken his game to a very high level,
Focuses solely on bettering himself and keeping out of trouble.
If you have never met him and don't know who he is,
Start getting acquainted with RAHEEM, PIIPE, FRANCIS.

REMEMBRANCE DAY

Once again, remembrance day is here,
When we celebrate the lives of those brave men and
women, who showed just how much they care.
They sought and they fought, for our great freedom,
I think that they all, are the real champions.

I may never know, what getting she'll shocked really feels like,
But imagine those who had to deal with it, for most of their lives.
They constantly heard the firing, of bullets and cannons,
Not to mention the terrifying sound, of a mortar bomb.

You only heard the bombs fire, but didn't know where they would land,
And whenever they made landfall, the explosion was very grand.
The helmets and vests, could only provide so much protection,
But a bullet from close range, could send you straight to hell or heaven.

Back in the days, they didn't have the M-16 rifle,
But only a powder filled musket, to go into battle.
They had to ready those barrels, and very quickly fill them with powder,
Because in the blink of an eye, the enemy got closer.

How many of us, would take up a weapon and leave our land,
Without even knowing, the evil thoughts of another man.
Those brave soldiers didn't know, what would become of them,
But all that was on their mind, was the safety
of their relatives and children.

All of the battles, were a fight to the finish,
And if one only hesitated, they would become a statistic.
For the life of a soldier, is never ever easy,
Imagine having to say to your spouse, one day well meet again baby.

Most of them left our country, not knowing if they would be back,
But it was for a very worthy cause, and that's a fact.
They gave up their lives, so that we could live ours today,
That's why all year long, should be remembrance day.

Some were very fortunate, to make it back to our shores,
And tell the tale of their fallen, sisters and
brothers who are with us no more.
So with every breath of life, in my body I'll say,
Put all of their names on the list, for National Heroes day.

Romaine Belgrove
13/11/2016

ROSE

Just the other day you were but a mere seedling,
But soon grew to be an awesome and super being.
For the 20 + years I never saw you hold a grudge,
Any sign of anger soon melted away like hot fudge.

I could remember the first day we ever spoke,
You, having interest in me seemed like a joke,
But as time went by I soon found you to be a true friend,
Who always had my back right down to your very end.

Not only did you have it just when you were a child,
But for all your life you carried that beautiful smile.
Giving it to everyone who came in contact with you,
No grey skies were too much for you to turn blue.

You were someone with pure positive vibes,
Who had a great impact on all our lives.
Whether it be during carnival playing mas,
Or right after a cricket game sitting with your girls on the grass.

You had a free spirit wherever you did roam,
But no matter what your heart was committed to home.
Your family and kids were your whole life,
Left up to you they would never see strife.

There are so many people whose lives you have touched,
And in return you never asked for much.
But just to be honest and truthful to you,
Because you're human and of course you have feelings too.

You'll not only be missed by your immediate
family and the village community,
But also by all members of the Out and Bad Boat Ride family.
Who will never understand but have to accept,
The fact that you already breathed your last breath.

To speak of your whole life, I'd have to write a story,
But am sure you're in a better place up high in glory.
Looking down on everyone wishing you were here,
To still bring us lots of laughter and good cheer.

In every flower garden one always stands out,
That was all you without a shadow of a doubt.
So, sleep on Rosemary Williams the name your mom chose,
But to me and others you'll always remain our beautiful ROSE.

Romaine Belgrove
10/10/2018

SANITATION DESERVES SALUTATION

You wake up every day, and get all nicely dressed,
And tend to forget about the ones, who clean up all your mess.
We too can also, dress up and go out,
But keeping our Country clean is mainly what we're about.

That doesn't mean, that you can just go around dropping your mess,
No that's unacceptable, even if you have on your Sunday best.
And it's even worse, when you look at us with laughter,
After you've just littered and say that's what we're there for.

We've committed ourselves to cleanliness, once we're alive,
You might try, but don't understand, what gives us that drive.
It's very easy, and doesn't need a special art,
Just think of the consequences, if you don't play your part.

If we all take some pride, and do what we're supposed to do,
Then you won't have to wonder, what it's like to walk in our shoe.
Because our shoes are very, very hard to fill,
Think of cleanliness, like a Sergeant Major conducting a drill.

Some sit back and wonder, how can we do a job like this,
And sometimes it seems as though from birth,
we were already chosen for it.
I must tell you also, that it's not an easy task,
It's not the tough times, but the tough people who last.

People always say, it's a dirty job but it must be done,
But when you look at us, it's always with great shun.
It doesn't really matter; we've now grown accustomed to that,
But instead of all ridicule, what about, a slight
pat of gratitude on our backs.

As you open your eyes daily, you meet a clean environment,
And you give all the high praises, to the government.
They're doing their part; now don't get me wrong,
But it's about time accolades go, to whom they rightfully belong.

It's always easier to pull down someone, than to raise them up high,
But we the sanitary workers do a very good job, and this you can't deny.
So, don't hold back, on giving us our congratulations,
Because after all, **SANITATION deserves
all the best SALUTATIONS.**

SENSITIZE, SANITIZE, STAY ALIVE

As life goes on diseases will come and diseases will go,
What makes the difference, is how much do you know.
Because all of a sudden on every street corner,
Everyone you know is now a nurse, or a doctor.

Every epidemic is always followed by rumors,
And what you choose to believe could save the life of you and yours.
So, don't go around believing everything you hear,
But instead stay tuned for when the health professionals are on the air.

The world as we know it will never ever be the same,
With the discovery of the virus also came the blaming game.
Because everyone is caught up, in whose fault it is,
But that won't cure, one of the world's deadliest viruses.

Some people say, that it was made by the Chinese,
While others are convinced, that the US is
trying to bring China to its knees.
Arguing about that, will never solve it,
Because we now have on our hands, a full-blown pandemic.

There will be restrictions and; also travel bans,
As everyone is trying hard to keep it out of their lands,
No one up to yet can come up with a cure,
While daily on the news, we see people falling to the floor.

It doesn't have to be your neighbor or your close friend,
We need to look out for each other right down to the end.
It's not picking out any class creed or race,
And this virus is moving at a rapid and deadly pace.

The supermarkets are all running out of toilet paper,
And everybody, is panicking about later.
Pushing, shoving and fighting each other still,
If the virus doesn't wipe us out, we ourselves will.

This is not the first and it surely will not be the last,
But like all other sickness and diseases, it will also pass
Whether it's called COVID 19 or CORONA VIRUS,
With God on our side, who or what can prosper against us.

Romaine Belgrove
22/03/2020

SIR S. W. TAPLEY SEATON

Have you ever seen someone so cool, calm and collective?
Who doesn't know how to take, but always willing to give?
Standing tall and very proud in stature,
It can clearly be seen that kindness is his nature.

Even before he took office, in his new position,
Just approach him respectfully and you'll have his attention.
Speaking in a soft and subtle voice that knows no anger,
Don't get it wrong he also has a side for humor.

Even if he's busy and tells you to wait a while,
When he's ready you'll be greeted by that big broad smile.
Making you feel comfortable like you can tell him anything,
He holds a good conversation that never gets boring.

Studying and enforcing law is also his passion,
He might not be as active now but he'll give you his opinion.
And even if, he just lost a hard, fought case,
The opponent would always be met with a warm embrace.

He now has personal security of very special rank,
But on any given day, you'll see him alone entering the bank.
To do his own transactions and it's not because of ill trust,
But merely being accustomed, to helping himself without a fuss.

His appointment in government came with a new prestigious home,
But I don't think he minds, when on his grass you're allowed to roam.
He's always willing, once possible to host an event,
Ask the Solid Waste workers, they were invited and all gladly went.

Don't think he's a pushover because he doesn't scream and shout,
If you violate his wishes, the guards will put you out.
And don't be fooled by the calmness and those glasses,
Am sure he always came out on top in all his classes.

Very well molded and rounded in every way,
We'll give him all his flowers that are due to him today.
So, join me in saluting him, and all with good reason.
He's our beloved Governor General **SIR S. W. TAPLEY SEATON**.

Romaine Belgrove
14/12/2018

ST. CHRISTOPHER CHILDREN'S HOME

Some of us, are not fortunate enough to have a family,
And the question is asked, why doesn't anybody want me.
That my dear children is not necessarily true,
Such a place exists with people who care about you.

These wonderful people toil day and night,
Just to make sure that you're all treated right.
They don't really ask, for too much in return,
Just that you attend school and do your chores when it's your turn.

You all are, like an extended family to them,
And all they're guilty of is loving you again and again.
I know that sometimes you won't like the decisions made,
But don't let that stop you, from excelling in your grades

This home is here to give you the chance you deserve,
Without you worrying about getting on the workers nerves.
Because they are trained to handle almost any situation,
And focus on making you, the future of our nation.

The institution had a great founder many years ago,
Who made sure that the kids were always on their toe
She was very firm and stood for no nonsense,
But just respect her and others and you could be best friends.

When church was over you had to pay special attention to her lips,
Because the only words you heard were, 'Beat the Bricks'.
Don't waste time and say, you're fixing your shoe,
Because it only got worse when she said, don't
let me reach home before you.

She didn't do it, to scare the children away,
But that discipline, is what made them so successful today.
It was a joy to see the boys well dressed and the girls with their purse,
We will never forget, such a wonderful lady we all called '**Nurse**'.

She left a legacy, that surely is being carried on,
In a place that cares deeply for the less fortunate as soon as they're born.
The workers never complain and say the kids are too many,
So, I think the Lord will bless them to see,
another seventy years times seventy.

Romaine Belgrove
25/01/2020

SUNRISE

When you wake up in the morning and open your eyes,
You should feel privileged to see another sunrise.
Because while you can celebrate, another day with your family,
Someone somewhere, wasn't quite as lucky.

To see the dew fall on the newly opened leaves,
Or the Majestic flight from flower to flower, of the honey bees.
All make a new day so spectacular,
And we just look on in awe and wonder.

A first glimpse of the ocean, looking calm and tranquil,
It's almost as if, the whole world is at a standstill.
The fishes are all, having a grand time,
Not even paying attention to the bait on that fishing line.

The blue sky, is now getting very bright,
Either by tiny rays, or a powerful glare of sunlight.
Bringing along with it the heat of a new morn,
Sleepy eyes are wishing, that it still was dawn.

The sea gulls and pelicans, now hover the sea,
Stalking their prey, unseen by the naked eyes of you and me.
The fishermen, are always paying attention to this,
Because wherever these birds gather, there's always plenty fish.

Always cherish the sunrise whenever you get a chance,
You never know, if that might be your last glance.
Because even though, you might not be
having the best night of your lives,
Your day just might be better, when it starts with a beautiful sunrise.

Romaine Belgrove
17/05/2020

SWMC

-1-
SWMC or Solid Waste Management
Corporation in case you didn't know,
First became a Legislative Act twenty years ago.
Even before that, it had been championing the cause,
And now it is written in the book of Laws.

-2-
The main duty is to spearhead the cleanliness of our Country,
But don't be fooled it still has a lot to do with you and me.
The Corporation functions 24-7 and 365,
And plays a major role in the cleanliness of our lives

-3-
Whenever there's a big function and all the
patrons have gone home to sleep,
That is the time when our sweepers have begun to clean and sweep.
They all have their own areas and work as a team,
And by the time the sun rises, our streets are sparkling clean.

-4-
As early as 4:00 a.m. the collection team goes at it,
And gets their job done before the start of our busy traffic
If your waste is collected, be it in the morning or evening,
You can count on the employees to be there
whether it's sun, rain or snowing.

What once ago, use to be called the dump,
Has been transformed into a place where you
can even sit and have your lunch.
No more do you have to worry about driving
through garbage and losing your tires.
But instead, there's a nicely paved road that
leads you straight to the scale tellers.

Whether it be little roller or a twelve cubic yard bin,
Just make the necessary arrangements and
watch the Rasta man do his thing.
You can rent for one day or have it for the weekend,
The choice is yours but the service provided
makes your money well spent.

If by chance you have one or more derelict,
Call us up and have it removed before our
Litter Wardens issue you a ticket.
They are very serious when it comes to their work,
So, don't try to mistreat them because the supervisors don't make joke.

Once you reach the office even if it's just for a little while,
The first thing to greet you is a warm smile.
Our staff deals with your business in a very professional way.
Once you're done with your business you have
no choice but to have a great day.

As with any organization there has to be someone in charge,
He might not be the biggest in body, but his decisions are large.
The way he runs the Corporation is unlike any other,
There will never be another like our General Manager,
MR. ALPHONSO BRIDGEWATER.

Romaine Belgrove
2016

TALK SUGAR TALK

Extra, extra read all about it,
It's the earth strong of the man with plenty class and wit.
You hear him talk about it all through the year,
Now finally, the bowl's birthday is here.

All of Freedom DJ's are good and this we all know,
But you're just unique on our beloved morning show.
Without even trying you give people things to talk about,
And you also get paid handsomely for banging you mouth

Radio disc jockey de man was born to be,
Always providing entertainment, for both you and me.
Does ads part time, and loves playing mas,
Because he put on a dress you vex, man you full a glass.

Just like Pringles, once you pop you can't stop.
Try to shame him, and you'll talk till you drop.
So, all those of you, trying to bad mind still.
His ignore button, ain't even half way up de hill.

Mighty Shorty, Leslie, or D Bowl, call him what you like,
He's one of those memories you never forget, just like riding a bike.
Guys are not in touch with their emotions, you always hear,
But look closely at him he's probably shedding a tear.

Just this morning we spoke and I told you I wouldn't write anything,
But I couldn't help it, you're a friend worth keeping.
And this is the way I choose to show my appreciation,
For brightening up my day even when it seems I faced my last one.

Romaine Belgrove
22nd November 2019

THE PERFECT MOTHER

Why are you struggling to be the perfect mother?
And we know when it comes to perfection, there is no other.
Than the one true God whom we serve up above,
And all He asks, is that you give abundant love.

There's no need to wonder, if you're doing it wrong or right,
Just keep pressing on, with all your might.
Always leaning, towards our Saviour,
You and your kids will never be in danger.

There is no handbook, on how to raise children,
Just do your best, and instill good values, again and again.
You're still human, and can get upset like a mad bull,
But once you pray to God, your thoughts remain calm and faithful.

Even when it seems, like you want to crack under pressure,
The look on your kids face, remind you that you're a mother.
That's when all negativity, begins to subside,
And love pours out, like water running down a slide.

Though a lot of technical jobs, are mostly done by men,
Modern day Era has paved the way for many women.
And we should all think of it, as something positive,
After all, who says a mother of five can't be innovative.

Gone are the days, when women stay at home in the kitchen,
But instead, we're now sharing the chores and the cooking.
And sometimes, the mother is the main bread winner,
Especially, in the unfortunate absence of the children's father.

When food is available, whether little or plenty,
Even if it's not her child, she won't leave them hungry.
Making sure, that each and every mouth gets full,
You can't deny, that the higher percentage of
mothers, are always thoughtful.

The world today, is moving swiftly ahead,
Please cherish your mother now, instead of
her memories when she's dead.
You can look from now until eternity, you won't find another,
She might not be perfect, but she's your one and only **mother**.

Romaine Belgrove
06/05/2020

TRIBUTE TO CLEMENT 'BOUNCIN' WILLIAMS

Seventy Years ago, you came to us and now you're not here,
And it's going to be extremely hard to not shed a tear.
Because you were someone whom we had no choice but to love,
And I am sure you're looking down on us all from above.

Very well educated and blessed in so many ways,
You'll surely be missed for the remainder of our days.
No problem was too hard for you to lend a helping hand,
And you were God's definition of a real man.

When you wrote those scripts, they were to be portrayed your way,
If not, one would hear, go home and come back another day.
Because your love, for theatrical art was so ardent,
That you came up with, the national players theater movement.

You didn't have to do much to gain some respect,
Because we knew what time it was when you took
a deep breath of that big broad chest.
So, one had no choice but to do as they were told,
Or the next practice session someone else would be playing your role.

Script after script and you never thought to retire,
From the things that many others never even had the desire.
I am not just talking about the science or performing arts life,
But also, the main focus which was your beautiful children and wife.

Helping others to get a good education was also your big interest,
Along with helping them to bring out their inner most best.
And when taught by you one had no choice but to learn,
Because when it comes to education you were very stern.

Although your large bodily stature would sometimes cause fear,
Deep down inside you were just like a cuddly bear.
Not using it for intimidation,
But to make others aware of a passionate situation.

Apart from your own loving biological family,
You had another which was anybody in the circus with a taxi.
You proved that you deserved their utmost love and respect,
A situation against which I would never bet.

So, what more can I say about you my dear friend,
Other than you were pleasantly loved always to the end.
All that was said is not just the flapping of gums,
But to pay special tribute to my friend and
yours, **Clement 'Bouncin' Williams.**

Romaine Belgrove
4th September 2018

TRIBUTE TO TONI FREDERICK

This fine lady is so full of burning desire,
That she has more zest, than a raging ball of fire.
When it comes to her work, she's serious but
also loves to have a lot of fun;
And from a good media challenge she will not run

Her Breakfast Club Show helps you start your day right;
you just have to love her with all your might.
There isn't a song or artiste that she can't find,
She has her own personal library stored in her mind.

Although most people are always talking about cash,
Her favourite topic is talking trash.
So, tune in to the program every Tuesday morning and get educated,
For you won't find another who, to this topic is so dedicated.

She is all about her Country and keeping it clean,
So, if she pulls you up about littering, don't think she's being mean.
Everyone at times can get a little bit sassy,
But she's so professional and always remains classy.

She has years of undying service to WINN FM 98.9,
I think she should be employee of the month until 2099.
When it comes to reporting, there isn't another
That can be so precise, be it news, sports or weather.

Be it working or relaxing she always wears a smile,
And whenever she passes, you must take a glimpse even for a little while.
So even if you think you're a lover of and you believe in magic,
Just wait until you meet this amazing lady called TONI FREDERICK.

Romaine Belgrove
12th July, 2016

TWIN WARRIORS OF GOD

You are truly blessed to be born into a family with other siblings,
But it seems even better when you realize you have a twin.
You don't have to be born of the same gender,
It is comforting enough to know that you always have each other.

You can like the same things, or you can just be different,
It doesn't really matter; you both have the same parents.
You both love music and also love to sing,
With God in your lives you can do just about anything.

Whenever Oshe Baba starts to play,
Tell yourself it's going to be a great day.
She not only joins in the singing,
But look at her unique movements when she does her thing.

Motown has some of the greatest dancers,
But I still don't think they have anything over her.
If you have never seen it before,
Look at her shoulders and feet as she glides across the floor.

Her brother Chesil was one of our calypso greats,
Whenever he was in competition, patrons tried hard, not to be late.
Because they knew it would be a very great show,
Once he held that mic to start his calypso.

He did battle, among some of the very best,
And he never got pompous or started beating his chest.
He was and still is, one of the greatest in our land,
But also such a unique and humble man

Worked at Social Security and helped us to help each other,
And has now hung up the pen and taken up the camera
Taking pictures, whenever he gets a chance,
Giving you breath taking views even if just for a glance

Nothing can alter their true faith in God,
Always praising him, even if it's just by a nod
Join me in saying happy 65th birthday to both warriors from Moravian,
Brother Chesil and his sister, Adelyn Hamilton

Romaine Belgrove
31/01/2020

UNCLE NORRIS

Our house on the Bay front, wasn't a mansion,
But it had the fondest memories, in my opinion,
And you were, at the forefront of all that,
When we touched your stuff, Momma would say, put it right back.

For you held a very special place in her heart,
When you contacted her, the cleaning would start.
There was not to be even a speck of dust,
Having a clean house for you, to her was a must.

We all knew when you were returning from the States,
Because out came those special teapot, cups, saucers and plates
It was always a pleasure to see you get treated so special,
That is living proof of everlasting love without denial.

It was always a mystery how you got such special care,
Even Kilene chipped in by plucking out your gray hair.
Oh no she didn't do it just because she thought it was fun
But she got her hands full of coins, when the job was done.

You didn't have to do much to get our attention,
Just pull across your room's curtain and all playing was done.
At the sound of your voice, we sometimes ran and hid with fear,
But we'd give anything to still have you here.

All who met you didn't have a choice,
But to fall in love with you, after you spoke with that clear subtle voice.
But don't be fooled and try to take you for a joke,
Because if necessary, you demanded respect when you spoke.

The saying is that we're promised three scores and ten,
You surpassed that figure, and did it again and again.
Always choosing to have Jesus as your guide,
And we hope that you're now, sitting right by his side.

You were a son, a father, a brother, but to most of us uncle,
And though it's a sad day we're still happy for you.
You can now continue your journey with Duchess and look down on us,
You'll forever be in our hearts **UNCLE NORRIS THOMAS**.

Romaine Belgrove
17/9/2019

UNOMA 'PHENOMENAL' ALLEN

From inception into this earth you were always destined to be,
An amazing woman with exceptional qualities
Simple, humble but yet also proud,
Always on the quiet side and never too loud

Among your classmates you always stood out,
Dealing with any situation without having to shout
While others focused on beauty and how they were dressed,
Your main goal was to pass all of your tests.

Always remaining among the top five,
With a positive spirit so vibrant and alive.
Never boasting of good grades or what you could do,
You said it all in your song, walk a mile in my shoe.

That would transform you into lady sunshine,
Competing with the veteran calypsonians, already in their prime
You managed to stand out, in that arena,
Just as you did in the arts of theater

Whether sending a message or acting a comedy,
Your involvement always helps out even one family.
And even though many might not approach you,
Are sure too many young people you are a role model.

When many thought there's nothing else you could do,
Proving them wrong, seems to be a habit with you,
Because you ventured into deep waters where many would only stand,
When at your age you entered the Miss Black San' Bangalang.

Am sure your family is overwhelmed with pleasure,
To see that a simple young lady turned into such a wonderful treasure
Never being rude or disrespectful to anyone,
But instead always being there as someone to count on.

In order to help others, you have found another way,
By now opening, the one and only soup Café
If by any chance there's question of who am talking.
She's the phenomenal one and only **UNOMA ALLEN**.

Romaine Belgrove
05/11/2018

UNSUNG HEROES

A very hard and tedious job is what we do,
But it's very important to the health of both me and you.
Can you imagine living, with garbage all over the place,
In my opinion we keep our country as clean as outer space.

Be it sun, rain, sleet or snow,
Each and every morning we're always on the go.
Even when we wake up with our body in pain,
Just look at our sweepers, still tidying up those drains.

It's already known, the pay isn't the best,
But our work is still always done, with pride and zest.
Many have come, and many have gone,
But no matter what, the work must go on.

The cleanliness of our country is now spreading
to more than just Kittitians,
We started out with all locals, but now we even have Jamaicans.
Because, sickness from germs and filth doesn't pick or choose,
And if not controlled, many lives we will lose.

We're not perfect and some workers can be very tricky,
Give them too much space and they become very slippery.
Deep down I know, that they still mean well,
But you also would try to run away if you're
job seemed like you were in hell.

You the patrons, sometimes reward us with goodies or even cash,
But please don't use that as a bribe, to throw
illegal stuff in between your trash.
Because when you think it's made right by your given dollar bill,
You only complicate the job, of the guys at the landfill.

As the title suggests we're the real unsung heroes,
Doing a job that always has us on our toes.
The country now has, a National Hero family,
So, Mr. Prime Minister, I think you know where
to look, for next year's nominee.

It's all good to hear the government say,
For this Christmas we'll double your pay.
We work so hard with very little praise,
The best gift of all, would be a happy New Year's raise.

Romaine Belgrove
13/12/2019

WASTE MATTERS

We have our beautiful Nation; and we say Country above self,
In keeping with that let's protect our health.
We all have only one life to live,
So instead of taking from our islands let us give.

You don't have to work at Solid Waste to know that waste matters,
For every piece of litter have consequences thereafter.
Whether a bag of garbage or just a candy wrapper.
Every time you litter, our own lives you endanger.

We all have to chip in and play our own part,
Because keeping a country clean is pride and not a skill or an art.
Dispose of your waste in the proper way,
Then you will give the authorities less things to say.

Don't just do it for a medal upon your chest,
But think about our Nation's progress.
Even though we are small and not recognized by many,
It's safe to say we have one of the cleanest countries.

To dump waste illegally is considered a crime,
And if this continues, we'll get left behind.
Many a tourist says they'll come back to our shores
Because of the cleanliness that greets them upon opening doors.

Managing waste is not a job for any one man
But instead we should all be working hand in hand,
So bag it and wrap it, and properly dispose of your garbage,
For then and only then our beautiful Federation
will be better than average.

Romaine Belgrove
2016

WHAT IS A MOTHER

What do you think of when you hear the word Mother?
You are probably saying, that's the woman who's
always nagging me and my brother,
But in any instance when you get right down to it,
You know for sure God knew what He was doing
when He gave man such a special gift.

Whether she's a biological Mother or not,
Next to Jesus, she's the dearest friend you've got.
So, no matter how many hills and valleys your feet may stride,
Your loving Mother is the ultimate tour guide.

They say there's nothing like a woman's scorn,
And am sure you started believing that when you
received your first spanking after you were born.
Because when she makes a swing and catches you in the hip,
Nothing can compare to when she says a word with every lick.

Sometimes you get fed up of her talking and think that she's a real stress,
But think of how she felt carrying you for nine
months or more without proper rest.
So whenever you're ready to argue and complain,
Just remember when you get in trouble, the
first thing you do is call her name.

You may not always think that her decisions are in your best interest,
But I know for sure, my Mother is always good, better, best.
Because all my life she has steered me in the right direction,
And no matter the circumstances, I wouldn't
trade her not even for a million.

You constantly scratched, kicked and punched her
when from her belly you wanted to get out,
And sometimes the pain got so overbearing she had to scream and shout.
But when all the bleeding, sweating and tears are over,
She would walk to the end of the earth and back
if anyone tries to take you from her.

There are some women, who have to be both Mother and Father,
So, before you even think of being disrespectful,
please use that as a gentle reminder.
Because she loves all her children unconditional and dearly,
And I'm sure at times you think she's living proof of the tooth fairy.

Every so often we all get a little side tracked,
But whatever the struggle, Mother dear always
has our front, sides and back.
So, when it's all said and done I always tip my hat to all Mothers,
And I won't wait until you die, but instead I must
while you're alive overwhelm you with flowers.

Romaine Belgrove
7th May 2016

WOMAN

It's said that God took a rib from Adam to create woman,
but by now they've already earned equality in my opinion.
Doing whatever is necessary to maintain that happy home,
I pray the lord would send one to those men living alone.

Her sole purpose is not to stay at home and clean,
but yet when she does it she's very keen.
When it's done don't you dare throw down your dirty shoes and socks,
Or else you just might find yourself on the other side of the door locks.

A woman should not be seen as a piece of meat,
because if that's your opinion you'll never get anything to eat.
Show them all respect, where it is due,
because as a man, you want the same shown to you.

We're into the age where women do just about everything,
so give them every encouragement, instead of discouraging.
Don't see it as a woman is now better at something than you,
but feel blessed that she can now bring in a large income too.

Success should be shared and not competed for,
we may not know it but that's part of God's law.
We praise him and say we're all a part of his family.
So why do you think the women should be less than you and me.

Women also had trials and troubles from since early days;
some were honored while some were beaten as slaves.
So don't think that struggles only happen to men,
it can clearly be seen, that is also shared by women.

There's a special day for just about any and everything,
so don't be afraid to acknowledge all women dead or living.
Because even though they might not be here with us today
they already played their part in paving the way.

Again I say take a good look at the world today,
And ask the lord to bless all women whenever you pray.
Showers of blessings should be given plenty,
so give a resounding applause, for international women's day 2020.

WOMEN OF FAITH

Some Organizations last and some don't, this we all know,
But we're still here standing from since 65 years ago.
Not by our own free will, but by the hand of the almighty,
Having our dull moments but also our triumphant glory

Ministering to both the old and young,
Our journey here on earth is never done.
Trying to save as many souls as possible,
Which we shall achieve with Christ as our handle

Doing the lord's will could sometimes be trying,
But we'll fight on with the well or the sick and shut in.
Never forsaking or leaving anyone behind,
No matter who or what we'll always find time.

We must press on as women of faith,
For one glorious day our reward will be great.
Not that we're doing it for anything in return,
But instead, just keeping with what we yearn.

So, come and celebrate with us women of God tonight,
Stand up and worship Him with all your might.
Then you'll see He'll take care of all your fears,
And give us another **Zion Women's Fellowship** of 65 more years.

Romaine Belgrove
26/10/2018